CONTENTS

BLOCK 4
ENGLISH AS ART

Diana Honeybone

INTRODUCTION

Block 3 introduced us to the study of English in action. We considered the different functions of the language, in its spoken and written forms, in everyday situations and for special purposes of work, trade or persuasion. The different cultural traditions of English speakers and writers were also an important part of our study.

We shall take these themes and concerns with us into Block 4, where we are going to examine a special function of spoken and written English: 'What makes English into art?' There will be some similarities with the topics encountered in the previous block, since you could argue that using English for creative purposes is a special way of putting it to work. On the other hand, we shall also be exploring the distinctive features of this special form of language use.

Week 14 opens up the question of why we regard some types of English as 'art'. It investigates how the sounds, meaning and grammar of English can be used to construct distinctive artistic effects, and how literary uses of language sometimes gain their impact by breaking generally accepted rules of language use. We begin to consider the role of the audience in interacting with the text. In week 15, we turn to more everyday uses of English, seeing how some of these features of 'literary' language are also present in the daily creative use of English in advertising, comedy routines, and other forms of 'popular culture'.

This leads us to the question of what constitutes 'great' literature. Where and how do we set the borderlines, and are these immutably fixed? Week 16 considers the question of the traditional canon of accepted great literary works and the criteria for choosing these; why should works composed in nonstandard varieties of English be excluded, for instance? Week 17 turns to the perspectives of writers, where different cultural and language backgrounds influence their attitudes to English and the ways they use it in their work.

THEMES

English in context
Block 4 looks at the geographical, social and cultural contexts in which writers produce their work, and in which audiences receive and interpret it.

Varieties of English
In Block 4 this theme is closely linked to context. We consider linguistic variation in 'English as art' – accents, dialects, codeswitching for literary effect. Variation is also related to function as we study the range of genres and styles in English literature.

Changing English
Since one of the ways in which literary English makes its impact is by its ability to surprise, there is a high rate of change in its styles and forms. We also consider the changing standards of what constitutes literature and whether the concept of a canon is itself outmoded.

Achieving things in English   In this block the emphasis is on English as a means through which creative writers achieve their aims of telling a story, conveying the emotional impact of an experience or simply entertaining. We look at the range of linguistic techniques they can use to gain their effects.

English and identity   This is an important theme of Block 4. It investigates the creation and exploration of a range of identities by writers in English through narrative and the 'voices' of dialogue. It also considers the positioning of the audience, who take on an identity as they interact with and interpret the text.

We shall draw, throughout the block, on a wide range of writings from Africa, India, Singapore and the Caribbean as well as from the USA and different regions of the UK. These will illustrate diverse forms of 'English as art' and the range of varieties of English used in literary writing. Such diversity will also lead us to consider how far there is agreement over what is accepted as 'art' and whether there are different interpretations and conventions in different contexts; we ask how far the acceptability and meaning of a work of literary art is negotiated between writer and reader in the light of their previous experience of other texts.

STUDYING BLOCK 4

To work through Block 4 you will need the following materials:
*   course book   *Using English: from conversation to canon*, Chapters 5–8
*   set book   *Describing Language*, Chapters 6 and 7
*   Audiocassette 4   Bands 1–6
*   Video   Band 4
*   TV 4
*   TMA 04   Options (a) and (b)

You will also be asked to carry out a number of practical activities and, as in previous blocks, we recommend that you keep a 'cuttings file' of your own examples of 'creative' language.

'Art' cuttings file

Cuttings that relate to Block 4 include any (preferably short!) examples of 'creative' language use or verbal play that you come across: a favourite poem, or songs; an advert that makes particularly striking use of language; puns, rhymes or riddles; perhaps certain forms of graffiti. It's useful to relate these to examples discussed in the course materials: see if the analyses discussed here apply also to your own examples, or if your examples add something new.

In addition to collecting written texts, you may like to note down any examples from radio or TV programmes such as comedies or plays. The commentaries of documentary programmes often use vivid descriptive language which makes use of verbal devices more often associated with literary uses of English. A further source of language play, in Britain at least, is names of shops and businesses which use puns – 'Mane Line' for a hairdresser; 'The Plaice to Eat' for a fish restaurant – which are relevant to Chapter 6. You can also add to your material on the topics you have already studied in Blocks 1, 2 and 3, and look out for anything relevant to children's use of language and to the use of English in education, ready for Blocks 5 and 6.

The chart below gives suggested timings for each week. We have tried not to overload the block itself in order to allow you time for a 'mid-course review' at the end of your study. We provide guidance on this below (p. 23).

Remember that the study timings can only be approximate, depending on your work rate. You will work through some components more quickly than we suggest, while others may take more time. As in earlier blocks, we advise you to spread your work for the TMA over more than one week; the workload of the later weeks in Block 4 is lighter than the first weeks', to allow for this.

Study material	Hours
Week 14	$10\frac{1}{2}$–$11\frac{1}{2}$
Week 15	$9\frac{1}{2}$–$10\frac{1}{2}$
Week 16	8–9
Week 17	9–10
Block review and TMA 04 (Options (a) or (b))	8
Mid-course review	2
Total	47–51

Study hint: before beginning work on Block 4 you should look at the questions and notes for TMA 04 Options (a) and (b) so that as you study you can assemble material to answer your preferred option.

WEEK 14   WHAT MAKES ENGLISH INTO ART?

Study questions

Questions	Related block themes
How does a writer foreground aspects of the form and structure of English to achieve artistic effects?	*Achieving things in English*
What uses can a writer make of dialogue, narrative structure and vernacular English?	*English and identity/ varieties of English/ changing English*
In what ways is a work of literary art influenced by the context in which it is created?	*English in context/English and identity*
How far is its meaning constructed by the context in which it is received by its audience?	*English in context/English and identity*

Introductory study notes and study chart

To work through this week, you will need these components, in the following order:

Study chart for course week 14

Course book		Set book			
Chapter/teaching text	Readings	Describing Language	Audiocassette 4	Video	TV
					TV 4 Animated English: the 'Creature Comforts' story
5 What makes English into art?	A In the vernacular				
	B Feminist theatre: performance language as art form and communicative gesture				
		7.4 Written language and 6.2 Non-verbal communication			
			Band 1 Introduction and Band 2 Spontaneous speech		
			Band 4 Story-telling		
Review of week 14					

Note: you are advised, if possible, to video-record TV 4 so that you can return to the programme in week 15.

This week's work marks the transition from Block 3's emphasis on uses of English for practical purposes – 'getting a job done' – to a different function of the language. We shall be exploring the nature of 'art' as expressed through the medium of words, whether written, as in a novel or a printed poem, or spoken, as in a play or poetry recital. We shall ask what features of English the creative writer can exploit to achieve the required artistic effect. Chapter 5 of the course book guides our study of the literary use of different linguistic features and considers the value of dialogue in both Standard and vernacular varieties of English.

This is backed up by an extract from Chapter 7 of *Describing Language* on the conventional structure of fictional narrative, and by Audiocassette 4 Band 2, in which we hear examples of two different ways of turning everyday language into 'art'. There is an obvious link between this and the work you did on everyday talk in week 10. Similar techniques of observation and selection created the script for

TV 4, 'Animated English: the "Creature Comforts" story'. We ask you to return to this programme later in Block 4, if you have been able to video-record it.

Context is an important theme in your study this week: we consider both the artist's social and cultural context and its effect on his or her work (a theme taken up more fully in week 17) and the reception of a work of verbal art by its audience within the context of their own experience. *Varieties* are also significant, in terms of the range of varieties of English available to writers and also the different genres within which they work; we see how both these aspects *change* with time and circumstances. We investigate how writers can construct *identities* for themselves by the styles they adopt and their use of other voices through narrative and dialogue – how the audience, too, is positioned in its identity as a participant interpreter – and how both work to *achieve* the aim of creating 'art' in spoken and written words.

The notes below will guide you through the components of this week's study, in the order in which they are given in the chart above.

TV 4   Animated English: the 'Creature Comforts' story

(Allow about 1 hour)

This programme connects with the discussion this week of how everyday talk may be adapted to make a script. It is based on a popular series of British TV advertisements for electrical power, which featured animated models of animals and birds using a script made from carefully edited talk in British regional accents. You will see the relevance of this programme to Audiocassette 4 Band 2 later in the week. There are detailed notes on TV 4 and some points to consider as you view the programme in the audiovisual notes at the end of this guide. Please turn to these notes now and read them, then watch TV 4.

Course book   Chapter 5 What makes English into art?

(Allow 6–7 hours)

This chapter opens up the issues of what differentiates language as art from other uses of language, and how we decide whether a particular written or spoken text should be classed as 'literature'. These topics will be developed further in later parts of Block 4, as we read and listen to the views of creative writers on their approaches to the use of the English language. Chapter 5 begins by introducing us to the linguistic and structural devices that a creative writer can use to tell a story, raise awareness of an issue, or recreate an emotional experience.

Here are some points to help you as you read:

- The chapter emphasizes the importance of an element of what is original, striking, even startling in the work of creative writers of English. This can be achieved in a range of ways which make us look at the subject matter in a new light. Section 5.2 begins with what may be familiar ground for students with an arts background: it draws on an aspect of linguistic analysis, *stylistics*, to help us in identifying the features of language which characterize the literary use of English. Bear in mind the concept of *foregrounding*, giving particular prominence to one of the inherent properties of English and so bringing it especially to our notice. We all use these features in everyday speech; for instance, popular sayings and clichés make use of *alliteration*: 'as bold as brass', and *rhyme*:'Red sky at night, shepherd's delight'. Section 5.4 points out how many authors base their style on the speech rhythms and imagery of their native cultural traditions. You can also link this back to the discussion in Block 1 of literary forms and techniques used in English in the past – for example, the use of alliteration and imagery in Old English verse (Chapter 3 in the first course book).

- One of the key issues we examine throughout this week is: what gives literary language its special quality and makes it different from everyday speech and writing? Part of the answer may lie in the conscious selection, arrangement and editing that result in an intensified use of language. The use of edited speech in a TV script has already been demonstrated in TV 4; Audiocassette 4 Band 2 will explain this further.

- Two closely linked elements of literary practice also help in the creation of a strikingly new use of language. The first is the deliberate breaking of the accepted rules of grammar by the author; all the rules governing the organization, pronunciation or written presentation of English are breakable, and to do so gives the reader a shock, whether small or large, agreeable or disturbing. It could be by one unusual word in a phrase, or by something more substantial. For example, if you know Lewis Carroll's poem 'Jabberwocky', do you recall the first time you met it and how you reacted to it? Look out for examples of rule breaking in the examples given in Block 4 and in your own personal reading. If you're a creative writer yourself, you could review your own poems and stories in the light of this chapter's ideas.

- A closely related element is the aspect of 'play' in literary writing. The author plays with words in unusual ways and combinations, and with a range of identities and viewpoints through narrative and dialogue, as section 5.3 points out. Week 15 will explore the playful use of language more deeply. Play can also be a serious matter (as it often is for young children) and the chapter, especially Reading B, shows how experimentation with forms of verbal and non-verbal expression can explore serious and important issues and intensify our concern about them.

- The theme of varieties of English is clearly present in the chapter. We consider the characteristics of the different genres of literature, and the individual uses of these genres by writers developing their own personal style. Look out also for the element of change, as conventional forms and styles lose their power to surprise and creative artists in English move on to develop new forms. Reading B has much to say about this process. Another element of variation is the use of vernacular forms of English, often with an element of the subversive attached to their use. Look at how the writer represents dialect in fiction; Reading A has some helpful discussion. You could compare these methods with the more strictly phonetic transcription described in Block 2 (particularly Chapter 7 of the first course book), and remind yourself of the social attitudes and values which are often connected with nonstandard varieties. (You have heard Tony Harrison reading one verse of his poem 'Them & [uz]' (mentioned in Chapter 5 of the course book) on Band 4 of Audiocassette 2. You may like to listen to it again in connection with this chapter.)

- A significant topic in the chapter is the creation of meaning in literature on many levels, including deliberate intertextual references to other familiar texts – section 5.4 explores this. We also think about the social and cultural context in which the author is writing. This will be more fully considered in the final week of this block, week 17. Section 5.4 also explores a crucial paradox for the audience's participatory role in responding to, and interpreting literature: each of us, as we read, listen or watch, responds in a way that is conditioned by our own cultural background, but the communication of our common human experience can reach across cultural divisions and have an impact on all of us. Reading B takes up this issue.

- One question that runs through the chapter, and is taken up by Audiocassette 4 Band 2, is where we draw our boundaries. How do we establish what is 'literary' use of language? See the notes on the cassette band in the audiovisual notes below for more discussion of this; the topic will also be raised in week 16.

Describing Language   Chapter 7, section 7.4

(Allow about 15 minutes)

This short section of the chapter follows the discussion of rhetorical structure that you looked at more closely in week 13. It analyses the formulaic structure of the typical traditional story, looking at elements of plot and grouping of characters. It examines some familiar stories, both folktales and modern TV episodes, to see how they fit this structure. This is relevant to our consideration of how literature is constructed. We have seen that the search for new forms can arise when familiar structures lose their power to surprise. The final section of this reading raises an alternative issue; we also need some connection to a recognized schema to help us to make sense of the story. Does literature need a combination of the startlingly new and the recognizable in order to succeed with its audience? Does this help us to understand why some highly original experimental work met with a hostile response when it first appeared?

Describing Language   Chapter 6, section 6.2

(Allow about 45 minutes)

This extract goes along with the discussion of non-verbal features of dramatic performance in Reading B in the course book chapter. It explains the range of non-verbal means of communication that we use, the impact these have on those we are speaking to and the ways in which they support and extend the spoken word. You may also like to look back at this point to Reading A of Chapter 4, which examined the use of non-verbal communication such as gaze and gesture by politicians making speeches, and to the comments on the body language of TV evangelists in Reading C of the same chapter. Another aspect of non-verbal support for verbal language is considered in week 15, on Audiocassette 4 Band 3, where you are asked to think about the interaction of music, words and performance in popular songs. Video Band 4, which you are asked to study towards the end of this week, also illustrates the importance of non-verbal behaviour in conveying a story.

Audiocassette 4   Band 1 Introduction to language and art

(Allow about 5 minutes)

This band introduces the cassette and the topics that it covers. There are no separate notes for this band.

Audiocassette 4   Band 2 The art of spontaneous speech

(Allow about 40 minutes)

This band examines further the use of everyday speech as the basis for art, and the processes of editing and selection that are necessary. Full notes on the band and an activity to accompany it appear at the end of this guide. Please turn to these notes now and read them, then listen to this band.

Video   Band 4 Storytelling

(Allow about 1 hour)

This band offers an example of language as art in the form of a traditional story, told by a storyteller to a live audience. We shall be asking you to analyse some aspects of the story this week and other aspects in week 15. Detailed notes to accompany this band are at the end of this guide. Please turn to these notes now and read through them. Then watch the band and work through this week's activities.

Review of week 14

(Allow about 45 minutes)

When you have worked through the audiovisual activities you have finished the work for week 14. Spend a short time now in reviewing what you have learnt by turning back to the study questions at the beginning of this week's study notes. Check that you can answer them and that you see the connection between this week's work and the themes of the course as a whole. You will then have a firm framework for the ideas and material that you will come across in the rest of Block 4.

WEEK 15   LANGUAGE PLAY IN ENGLISH

Study questions

These questions will help you to focus your thoughts as you work through this week's study material. We suggest that you keep them in mind as you work, and return to them when you review your work at the end of this study week.

Questions	Related block themes
What are the similarities and differences between popular language play and the literary use of English?	*Varieties of English/ achieving things in English*
What are the distinctive features of each form of language play, and what features do they share?	*Varieties of English*
How important are social and cultural contexts in influencing the form of popular language play?	*English in context/ English and identity*
How does the physical realization of language play affect its form and content?	*Varieties of English/ achieving things in English*

Introductory study notes and study chart

These are the materials that you will need for this week's study, in the recommended order of study.

Study chart for course week 15

Course book				
Chapter/teaching text	Readings	Audiocassette 4	Video	TV
6 Language play in English	A Songs in Singlish			
	B Social issues on walls: graffiti in university lavatories			
		Band 3 English in popular song		
				TV 4 Animated English: the 'Creature Comforts' story
		Band 4 Storytelling		
Review of week 15				

Note: if you were able to record TV 4 you are advised to review it during this week. Otherwise, you could look back through the TV 4 notes and your own notes on the programme.

This week we take up again the theme of 'language as play' which was one of the concerns of last week. The chapter of the course book and the associated band of Audiocassette 4 develop this topic, giving us the opportunity to explore in more detail the popular use and enjoyment of creative language play in everyday discourse. We consider five specific examples: comedy routines, popular song, graffiti, newspaper headlines and advertisements. As you work through this week, you can construct useful comparisons with week 10's discussion of everyday conversation and week 11's investigation of our everyday literacy practices – you could argue that our reading of advertisements and graffiti is part of our day-to-day literacy practices, anyway. You will also be aware of the similarities and differences between such 'popular' uses of language and the literary uses discussed in the other weeks of this block.

Varieties of English is a significant theme this week, as we consider the different forms and genres of popular language play and the *changes* that take place in their use. *Context* is also important – both the physical context of different forms of graffiti and the social and cultural context which affects a song's form or the intelligibility of a comedy routine. The worldwide enjoyment and use of these popular genres is reflected in the diversity of forms they take; we include material from Singapore, Nigeria and India as well as from the various strands of western tradition in the USA and Britain. The construction and adoption of *identities* by the contributors to these discourses is also our concern in this section and, as we read and listen to their productions, we shall be able to judge how far they have *achieved* their aim (of producing pleasure, amusement – or maybe irritation) through their use of language.

The notes below will guide you through the components of this week's study, in the order in which they are given above. Read the relevant study notes as you work through each component.

Course book   Chapter 6 Language play in English

(Allow 6–7 hours)

This chapter is the main focus of this week's work. The audiovisual material integrates with it; we recommend that you listen to Audiocassette 4 Band 3 in connection with section 6.3 of the chapter, as it illustrates the songs discussed in the section (see the separate audiovisual notes on Band 3 at the end of this guide). When you come to section 6.7, you should look again at TV 4 for a more detailed study of advertisements.

Here are some suggestions to help in your reading:

- One of the important questions posed by the chapter is, 'Why do we value language play so highly when it serves little practical purpose?' Ask yourself this as you work through this chapter; see how many of the examples you enjoy, and which you prefer (although this could tell you more about your own sense of humour than about the general acceptability of language play). One of the aspects of language play that appeals to all of us is its creative nature; look for the ways in which this operates as you study the different genres of popular language play.

- Look also at the range of ways in which the examples are used. For example, which ones are responded to by the general public as an audience but practised by professional experts, and which are open to anyone to practise? Perhaps you could also consider the element of improvisation in popular language art as a way of distinguishing it from what is accepted as literature. If you enjoy music, as a listener or performer, you could compare this with the amount of improvisation allowed or even encouraged in the musical traditions of different cultures and periods. The range of contexts is also significant; think about the importance of performance in some genres and how this can affect both form and message.

- A major preoccupation of this chapter is the effect of puns and word play, where humorous effect depends on a close similarity of form but a diversity in meaning between two or more words. This is discussed in many of the sections as well as in 6.6, which is devoted to it; you will find references in section 6.4, on graffiti, in section 6.5 on newspapers and in section 6.7 on advertisements. (You will have noticed the puns in the titles of the sections themselves.) It is useful to compare these references with the discussion of puns in literature in Chapter 5, section 5.2. If you are familiar with a language other than English, ask yourself what part puns play in that language, and how far it is possible to create cross-linguistic puns. Once we start to learn another language, we become aware of the difficulty of trying to translate verbal puns, since the similarities on which the joke depends are often a feature of the first language only. Does this help to explain something of the exclusive, culture-related nature of some popular humour? Think also about its transient nature because of the references to current events and features of a culture's life-style at one particular moment.

- Advertisements receive a detailed treatment in section 6.7, as well as in TV 4. When you have read this section and (if possible) watched TV 4 again, ask yourself how the techniques and formal features of advertisements compare with those of literature, with which they share many similarities (see week 14). You could also make a comparison with the forms of rhetoric you studied in week 13 – both aim to persuade, so how do they set about it? Is there a difference in the audiences they aim at?

- Finally, you will have become aware of the subversive element in much popular language art, from the protest songs of the 1960s to the political graffiti in student lavatories in Nigeria. Is this connected with the nature of play itself, as opposed to the seriousness of work? Does it reflect on the formal features of language play in breaking the accepted rules of grammar and so defying the 'official' patterns of behaviour? On the other hand, do all the users of popular language play have this subversive aim, or are some of them using these forms to gain the public's acceptance of a point of view (e.g. headline writers, advertisers)?

Audiocassette 4   Band 3 English in popular song

(Allow about 45 minutes)

This band extends the discussion of the use of English to produce popular language art in the words of a range of popular songs from the 1940s to the 1990s. They are drawn from different examples of this genre, and raise interesting questions about the varieties of English used and the relative importance in a song of words, music and performance.

Listen to this band as you work through section 6.3. It is a good idea to listen to the cassette before reading the section, as one of the songs played on the band is analysed in detail in section 6.3. You will find more detailed guidance notes and information about the songs included on it at the end of this guide; turn to these notes now and listen to Band 3.

TV 4   Animated English: the 'Creature Comforts' story

(Allow about 30 minutes)

After you have worked through section 6.7 of the chapter, the section dealing with advertisements, it would be very useful to review this programme. If you have not recorded it, look back at the notes you made while watching it. Also refer to the discussion of the programme in the audiovisual notes at the end of this study guide, and attempt the week 15 activity suggested there.

Video   Band 4 Storytelling

(Allow about 1 hour 30 minutes)

This band is also relevant to this week's study. Please turn to the video notes at the end of this guide and work through the week 15 activities.

Review of week 15

(Allow about 45 minutes)

In order to bring together the main issues and themes of week 15, look back to the study questions at the start of the notes for this week. Check that you can answer them and that you see how the course themes are reflected in the topics you have studied. This would also be a good point to look again at TMA 04 Options (a) and (b). Are you able to relate your work this week, and in week 14, to the TMA? You may be in a position now to select the option you wish to answer, but do try to think about both options. Reflecting on the *kinds* of question that can be asked about this material is a good way of helping to revise your work.

WEEK 16   AN ENGLISH CANON?

Study questions

These questions will help you to focus on the main points of this week's study material, and to sum up your conclusions at the end of the week. Keep them in mind as you work, and use them as part of your review.

Questions	Related block themes
How and why is a literary canon created, and by whom?	*Varieties of English/ English and identity*
What purposes can it be said to serve?	*Achieving things in English/English and identity*
On what grounds has the traditional English canon been challenged?	*English in context/ changing English/English and identity*
What suggestions have been made for replacing it?	*Varieties of English/ changing English*

Introductory study notes and study chart

These are the components that you will need for this week's work, in the order in which you will need to use them. Study notes for each component will be given in this order.

Study chart for course week 16

Course book		
Chapter/teaching text	Readings	Audiocassette 4
7 An English canon?	A English in the Caribbean: notes on nation language and poetry	
	B Hegemony and literary tradition in the United States	
		Band 4 The English canon
Review of week 16		

Blocks 1 and 2 have opened up the debate on standardization of language and the acceptability of certain varieties of spoken English. We are now going to ask similar questions about language as art, and to look at why some creative writing in English is, or has been, judged as 'suitable' for study, while other writing has been excluded.

This is to some extent a question of borderlines. It connects with the *varieties* of English used for literary purposes (a topic considered in Chapter 5 and one of the concerns of Chapter 8), asking whether some of them are more acceptable than others, and if so, why, and by whose standards. The *context* of literature is another related theme: do we take it into account when reading a literary work, or not? What part does the context play in determining the work's acceptability as literature? We examine the nature of the *identity* granted to writers whose works are included in a canon – and the identity granted to readers. The theme of *change* forms a vital part of this week's discussion; we consider changes in the canon, and even in the acceptability of the canon itself; we look at changes in social values that have altered attitudes to the study of literature, and at changes to literary forms themselves.

> *Study hint*: it would be useful to relate your work during this week to some of your earlier study – in particular week 4, which focused on standardization of language. Chapter 4 of the first course book contains a discussion of the rise of 'literary English' (pp. 141–8), as well as a brief discussion of 'dialect literature' (pp. 162–3). Much of the discussion here applies to a period that predates the establishment of a literary canon, but there were clearly strong views about what constituted 'good' and 'bad' writing.

The notes below will take you through the components of the week's work; read the relevant study notes as you work through each item. This week's workload is not very heavy and should allow you time to begin work on TMA 04.

Course book   Chapter 7 An English canon?

(Allow 6–7 hours)

Here are some suggestions to help you as you read this chapter. Band 4 on the audiocassette provides further examples of different views of the literary canon.

- As suggested above, this chapter has strong connections both with previous blocks of the course and with study material yet to come. We have already looked at the standardization of language in Blocks 1 and 2, and the implications of this for other varieties of the language. We have seen the connection with issues of power and authority, and with the exclusiveness that is an inevitable part of the adoption of one form as socially acceptable and prestigious. This chapter explores the same pressures on literature, this time consciously and deliberately applied by 'authorities' of literary criticism. There is further helpful material on vernacular English in literature in Chapter 8 of the course book, and on Audiocassette 4 Band 5, both of which you come to in the following week.

- The re-evaluation of the traditional canon and of the concept of having a canon at all can be a demanding and challenging process, especially for anyone who has grown up with the idea of a canon and has enjoyed canonical literature. Remember that such a challenge does not necessarily entail discarding all the contents of the traditional canon as worthless. It does mean looking again at how we define 'literature' and considering that a literary work may not be equally relevant to all readers of English, whatever their cultural context. It also means that varieties of English other than a standard variety may be a more suitable vehicle for the experience and message of a writer. It is not really appropriate for a course on the English language to pursue too deeply the question 'what is literature?' but if you are interested, there are some courses in the Arts Faculty which will allow you to take your interest further.

- We also consider the proposals of alternatives to replace the traditional canon. These range from moderate reform to radical rethinking. Does Chapter 6 of the course book throw any light on some of the alternatives? How far should popular culture be included in the study of literary uses of language, as some proposers suggest?

- Two important theoretical approaches to the study of literature are offered in this chapter; they have strong connections with the above points. One is Bakhtin's idea of the *centrifugal* and *centripetal* tendencies in language – the centralizing, standardizing force and the drive towards diversity and variation. The second is the poststructural emphasis on the joint creation of meaning in a text, through the reader's culturally based interpretation of the writer's words. Look at the attacks on the canon, and the defences of it, in the light of these views: how do the arguments offered fit with your experience as a reader of literature?

Audiocassette 4   Band 4 The English canon

(Allow about 40 minutes)

The band will help to explain three contrasting viewpoints on the question of what sort of canon we should have, if any. The audiovisual notes at the end of this guide will give you full information on the speakers and offer a study activity that will help you to identify their views. Read the audiovisual notes now and then listen to this band.

Review of week 16

(Allow about 1 hour 20 minutes)

The final activity in Chapter 7 of the course book asked you to consider your own views on the literary canon. We suggest you build on this activity as a way of reviewing your work during this week.

Chapter 7 included lists of books and authors suggested by three different people as appropriate for 'reading lists' for contexts with which they were familiar.

- Which ten books (or authors) would you suggest as important, or even essential, reading for someone growing up in a context with which you are familiar?

- How closely does your selection relate to the context you are thinking about (i.e. would some items in your list have much wider relevance)?

- How easy did you find it to make such a brief selection – and how comfortable are you with your final list? (S.K. Verma, from the Central Institute of English and Foreign Languages in Hyderabad in India, originally wanted to include a much longer list, but agreed to pare this down for the course book. His complete list is reproduced below.)

- If you can, ask two or three people you know to complete the same exercise. Try to choose people who differ from you and from each other in some respect – e.g. who are older, or younger, or who have different interests or lifestyles. How do their selections differ? How do you think these differences may be explained?

Complete list of authors suggested by S.K. Verma

1	Ernest Hemingway	24	Virginia Woolf
2	Somerset Maugham	25	G.B. Shaw
3	O. Henry	26	E.M. Forster
4	Christopher Fry	27	Harold Pinter
5	William Golding	28	André Gide
6	Robert Frost	29	Jean-Paul Sartre
7	Philip Larkin	30	Franz Kafka
8	W.H. Auden	31	Henrik Ibsen
9	Stephen Spender	32	Anton Chekhov
10	William Shakespeare	33	Henry James
11	William Wordsworth	34	Saul Bellow
12	S.T. Coleridge	35	Sylvia Plath
13	P.B. Shelley	36	Arthur Miller
14	John Keats	37	John Steinbeck
15	W.B. Yeats	38	Raja Rao
16	Aurobindo Ghosh	39	Jawaharlal Nehru
17	Jane Austen	40	Kamala Markandaya
18	Emily Brontë	41	Manohar Malgonkar
19	Charles Dickens	42	Patrick White
20	A. Tennyson	43	Mulk Raj Anand
21	R. Browning	44	Rabindranath Tagore
22	Thomas Hardy	45	R.K. Narayan
23	T.S. Eliot		

Think back to some of the other examples of creative writing or speaking discussed in this block and the previous one: how many of these might be admitted to a canon of one form or another? For example, think of the story told by Jan Blake on Band 4 of the video. Would a story that was:

- spoken rather than written
- based on a traditional folk tale
- told in a nonstandard variety of English

be admissible within your own view of a canon?

To consolidate this week's work, we recommend that you now turn back to the study questions at the start of this week's notes and look at them again. Jot down brief answers to them, checking that you can see how your points relate to the themes of the course. You will then be ready to go on to the last section of Block 4.

TMA 04

It is useful to begin working on your TMA during this week. If you can, choose the option you would prefer to answer, sketch out a rough structure for your assignment and begin assembling relevant material from weeks 14–16 under each heading.

WEEK 17   A TONGUE, FOR SIGHING

Study questions

These questions will help you in summing up your thoughts as you work through this week's study material and give a focus for your review at the end of the week.

Questions	Related block themes
What forms of English were chosen by the writers discussed in week 17, and what factors influenced their decision?	*English and identity/ English in context/ changing English*
What effect did these choices have on the form and expression of their writings?	*Varieties of English/ achieving things in English*
To what extent is tension between Standard English and another variety of English a significant feature in their work?	*English and identity/ English in context*
How far do they write as individuals and how far as representatives of a cultural group?	*English and identity/ English in context*

Introductory study notes and study chart

These are the components you will need in working through this study week; we recommend that you work through them in the order shown in the chart.

Study chart for course week 17

Course book			
Chapter/teaching text	Readings	Audiocassette 4	Video
8 A tongue, for sighing	A *The Language of African Literature*		
	B *Arrow of God*		
	C *Finding the Centre*		
	D *The Woman Warrior*		
	E *Lost in Translation*		
	F *The Murmur of Malvern*		
		Band 5 A tongue, for sighing	
			Band 4 Storytelling
		Band 6 *Lost in Translation*	
Review of week 17			
Review of Block 4			
Mid-course review			

The final week of Block 4 maintains the theme of the use of English as art. It moves on from last week's work on the canon, which was concerned with the study of literature in English and the criteria by which we determine which writings are to be studied. We now turn our attention from the students of literature to the writers themselves; we read and listen to what they have to say about the use they make of English and their attitudes to it as a language in which to express what they want to say. You will meet a range of attitudes to the choice of form as you work through this week.

Many of the now familiar course themes will surface as you work through this week's material. *Identity*, as an individual, a writer and a member of a social and cultural group, is a vital theme of many writers' contributions; the *context* from which they come and about which they write, and the context of the audience they have in mind, is connected to this. The *varieties* of English they choose to use – nonstandard dialects, creoles, Standard English, representations of codeswitching – each have a significance for what they say, and they will form an important theme of our study. We shall also become aware of the *changes* in attitude to the use of the vernacular as a literary medium, and the ways in which writers choose different linguistic strategies, as a result of their experiences of English, for *achieving* their aims and communicating what they want to say.

The notes below will take you through the components of this study week's work, in the order in which they are given above. Read the relevant study notes as you work through each component.

Course book   Chapter 8 A tongue, for sighing

(Allow 6–7 hours)

The distinctive title of this chapter, a quotation from Chinua Achebe, whose writing is discussed in section 8.3, picks out one of the main approaches of the chapter: the impact of English as a tool of colonialism. We consider how colonized people's language practices and cultural life, in which oral literature played a vital part (see the notes on Video Band 4, at the end of this study guide), were undervalued in comparison with the 'official' language of English; look at the comments by African writers in sections 8.2 and 8.3. This produces something of a dilemma, more so for a writer, whose communicative medium is words, than for other creative artists: which language shall be chosen as the means of writing? Ngũgĩ wa Thiong'o and Achebe both face the same dilemma, but choose opposing solutions – look at their reasons for doing so, and consider Jane Miller's point in section 8.4 that 'attitudes to language are always political'.

> *Study hint*: it will be helpful for your study of the course as a whole to relate your work in this week to earlier parts of the course. Look back to Block 1 (week 5) to remind yourself of the spread of English to British colonies in previous centuries. Think also of your study of Bakhtin in week 16 (Chapter 7 of the course book). What is the relevance of Bakhtin's views on the centrifugal and centripetal tendencies of language and the results of these for the two sides in this debate?

- In accepting English as his literary medium, Achebe does not take on all the cultural 'baggage' of the western world. You will consider, in Block 8, the increasing role of English as a 'global' language. Here, we investigate its use as an international 'voice' for writers to speak to a worldwide audience. You will hear the same point made by David Rubadira, an East African poet, on Audiocassette 4 Band 5. This view is held equally firmly by R.K. Narayan, an Indian author writing in English, when he says, 'We are not attempting to write Anglo-Saxon English' (section 8.5). You will notice how all of these writers give their English the cultural overtones, and often the structural features, of their own culture and language. As you read the extracts, you can differentiate between those who use Standard English, for narration, with different varieties as part of the dialogue between characters, and those whose narrative style is influenced by the rhythms and patterns of a language other than English or by a particular local variety of English.

- As Stuart Hall points out on Audiocassette 4 Band 4, colonialism left some cultures with no choice but to use a form of English. Writers from these countries face a similar problem in choosing a literary language, because their local variety of English, which reflects the personal experiences they want to write about, is not the Standard English taught in schools. You will notice, throughout the chapter and the cassette band, an emphasis on the tension between the language of the home background and the taught language of school. This is felt by writers in Britain too – look at Seamus Heaney's comments and listen to Liz Lochhead and Tony Harrison on the tape. Their choice, and that of many Caribbean poets, to mirror their experience in their home variety of English, has produced a great diversity of literary Englishes, as this week's study material illustrates. Consider also how this choice gives them an identity as a writer. Do the comments made by these writers reflect any aspect of your own experience in using English? Think also about the discussions of the nature of the canon; how does the work of such writers fit with the views that you studied in week 16 on what constitutes literature?

- For some writers, especially those whose learning of English was as a result of immigration, the adoption of this new language can mirror their isolation, or offer an escape from isolation. Read and listen to Eva Hoffman explaining her deliberate choice of English as the medium in which to create her writer's identity. Compare her views with those of other writers whose views are discussed in this chapter, who feel that the post-colonial experience of writers coming to terms with English makes them into 'exiles', caught between two cultures. Look at the statement of this by Spivak in section 8.7; she feels that her gender intensifies this problem. Is this a universal feeling, though? Hoffman integrated herself into her new language so that she felt at home in it; you can also compare Jaya's comment on her two cultures on Audiocassette 3 Band 5.

- The dialogic and intertextual nature of literature is picked up particularly in Heaney's comments in Reading F, but it is also present in other writers' views. The 'dialogue' that is foregrounded here is produced by the constant echoes of the language and literary forms of both the writer's own culture and the traditionally accepted 'literary' texts that these writers are moving away from.

Section 8.6 points out one unexpected result of the colonial introduction of English into India: some of the best writers in English at the moment are Indians, sometimes using an Indian variety of English. The same could be said of many writers and poets in former English colonies, who choose to use a local variety of English for their writing. Think of this when you come to the final blocks of the course, which will consider possible future developments in English.

Audiocassette 4   Band 5 A tongue, for sighing and
Audiocassette 4   Band 6 *Lost in Translation*

(Allow about 55 minutes and 25 minutes)

These bands extend the discussion in the chapter. We hear a wide range of writers who use English for their work demonstrating their reactions to standard literary English. You will find full details of the speakers and the extracts they read from their work in the audiovisual notes at the end of this guide. On Audiocassette 4 Band 5 some writers comment on what English means to them as a vehicle for literary writing. Others read their poems, in nonstandard varieties or local Englishes, and we compare their work with the varieties used by Jan Blake on Video Band 4. Band 6 is a more extended interview with Eva Hoffman, whom you have already met in Chapter 8; she reads extracts from her work, and talks about her early attempts to write in English.

Please turn to the audiovisual notes now, and use them to help you as you listen to these two bands.

Review of week 17

(Allow about 40 minutes)

To ensure that you have a clear understanding of the views on the use of English expressed in this week's material, turn back to the study questions at the beginning of this week's study notes.

Spend a few moments jotting down answers to them, noting how the points you make relate to the themes of the course.

The notes below suggest how you can review your work on Block 4 as a whole; and then, since you have reached the mid-point in your study we suggest you spend time on a more extensive review of your work so far on the course.

REVIEW OF BLOCK 4

(Allow about 1 hour)

To bring together the work of this whole four-week block, we suggest three brief activities.

Block 4 themes and questions

You will be familiar with this process from previous blocks. Turn back to the beginning of this study guide. Read through the introduction to the block again and look at the summary of the block's themes and how they apply to the material of Block 4. Check that you are aware of the presence of these essential themes in the material you have studied. Use the study questions at the start of each study week and any notes you have made in answer to them, to help you in this process.

Analysing literary English

Now we shall extend our practical application of the theoretical approaches of Block 4. Choose one of the extracts of literary material that Block 4 has offered you; read it through again and make notes on how it uses language to achieve its effects. You could look at one of the poems from Audiocassette 4 Band 5 – two of them are printed in the audiovisual notes at the end of this guide. You may like to make your own transcription of one of the others on Band 5, or choose the words of a song from Band 3, 'Eleanor Rigby', for example; you could take one of the extracts from novels discussed in Chapter 5 or Chapter 8 – one that has not been discussed in very much detail – and take the analysis further.

Use the guidelines set out in Chapter 5 of the course book and the related study notes to help you; there is also some helpful material in Chapters 6 and 8. You may already be familiar with similar activities from studying other courses with an element of literature; here, we shall be asking you to put rather more emphasis on the relationships between the written material and the choice of language and variety of English in which it is written, in accordance with the themes of this course.

For your selected poem or extract:

- Think about the writer's intentions – e.g. to tell a story, to convey an atmosphere, to put across a point of view; perhaps he or she is doing several things at once.

- Look at the choice of words – is there any emphasis on multiple meanings? Are words used literally or in a metaphorical sense? How is the impact of an individual word modified by the context of the surrounding words? Are there any elements of 'language play' – puns, for example?

- Look at the choice of linguistic features to achieve the writer's effects – alliteration, similar or identical sounds to create rhymes, use of the stress patterns of the language to create a rhythm – you can probably think of others.

- Consider the arrangement of words on the page: the lines of poetry, the different sentence lengths of prose, and the structure of conversation and narrative.

- Think about the register of the language – is it drawn from everyday speech? Are the words familiar or unusual, or a mixture of both?

- Look at the variety (or varieties) of English that the writer uses. Is it Standard English or a nonstandard variety? Does the writer switch from one to another? If so, what is the effect of this? Why do you think this variety has been chosen?

- Finally, taking all of these into account, would this poem or extract fit into any, or all, of the definitions of a 'canon' as set out in week 16?

Analysing your own examples

For the third activity in this section, turn back briefly to the note about the contents of this block's 'cuttings file' in the introduction. If you have been able to collect any material related to 'language as art', examine what you have collected in the light of the ideas and views put forward in Block 4. If you have included poems, extracts from fiction or song lyrics, you could analyse one or two of them along the lines suggested above, and compare them with the examples that you have already analysed. Would they be acceptable as contents of any of the canons discussed in week 16?

MID-COURSE REVIEW

(Allow about 2 hours)
There are two elements to this review.

General review

You are now half-way through the course. Although you will be busy with TMA 04 at the end of Block 4, it will be very helpful for your overall progress through the course if you can pause a little, before you go on to Block 5, and look back over your work so far. This will help you to consolidate your understanding of the ideas, theories and linguistic processes that you have met in Blocks 1–4. We certainly don't suggest that you re-read all the course material at this stage. Just look back at the summary of the course themes in the guide to week 1, to ensure that you are aware of each of them and of how they fit together. Then glance at the study questions for each study week, and at the brief notes that you made in answer to them.

This process should bring together what you have learned so far about the history of English in England and its spread to other countries; about the structure of the language, the different varieties of English and the effects these can have on listeners/readers; about the uses of English for social and work purposes, to get things done, to persuade, to amuse and to create literature. You will be beginning to realize how all these topics, and the course themes, relate to each other. As this is a complex process, a little time spent now in reviewing Blocks 1–4 will help to clarify the ideas addressed so far and give you a good, firm base from which to move on to the remaining blocks of the course.

There is the added bonus that your review will help in the (eventual) revision process for the examination. At the end of the course, you will have to go back over these blocks; a brief review now will make this final revision much quicker and easier.

Language and context

Now we would like you to concentrate on one of the major themes of the course, that of the *relationship between language and context*. It has been important in the course so far and will come into further prominence in the coming blocks, so this is a good point at which to look at its place in our study of English. Turn back again to each of Blocks 1–4 in turn, this time focusing on the material connected with the context in which language is used, and its influence on the form, register and variety used in particular circumstances.

You will find plenty of indicators in the study guides to help you. Use the introductions and theme summaries in each block, the introductions and study questions to each week and the study notes to each chapter. Context is a more significant element in some study weeks than in others; the study notes should help you to decide which areas of the material to spend time on. Make brief notes on the *kinds* of context featured in each block, and the *effects* they have on the use of English. These will provide a useful reference file on this important area of the course and lay the foundation for your investigation into the influence of context in English in the second half of the course.

Some points to help you:

• Context can be social, cultural, geographical – perhaps you can add to this list; sometimes more than one contextual factor is operating at the same time.

- In Block 1 look for the importance of social and cultural factors in the historical development of English, in its use by different groups at particular periods in its history and in the changes that occurred in its form, role and position in relation to other languages. You could also consider the contexts that produced the different 'stories' of English that Block 1 discusses.

- In Block 2 you will find most material in week 8, which examines stylistic or 'contextual' variation in English, and the influence of context on where, how and when codeswitching takes place.

- Block 3 puts considerable emphasis on context; re-examine Chapters 1 and 2 for the influence of context on everyday speech and literacy practices. Consider the specialized forms and registers of English that are used in the range of contexts connected with work and with public speaking. Also ask yourself how important context is in the methods used in analysing language; look again at conversation analysis – turn back to *Describing Language* Chapter 7, section 7.3, if you like, to remind yourself about this.

- Block 4 also has some useful material. In week 14, consider the contexts in which literature is written, the audience for whom it is intended and the social and cultural influences on the writer. In week 15, look at the influence of context in determining the acceptability of different forms of language as 'play'; this is backed up by weeks 16 and 17 – how far is the concept of a canon, and the form that this takes, dependent on context? You could ask yourself how far the work of a creative writer is determined by the existing social and cultural context; are there examples of writers deliberately setting out to subvert or break down existing expectations and so create a new context for the reception of their work? This brings us to the question of how context is established and maintained, how it is modified and what impact such modifications have on the use and forms of English.

As you move on into the second half of the course, keep on looking for evidence of the influence of context on English.

AUDIOVISUAL NOTES

TV 4   ANIMATED ENGLISH: THE 'CREATURE COMFORTS' STORY

Producer: *Paul Manners*
Academic consultant: *Neil Mercer*
(Duration: 24 minutes; study times: allow about 30 minutes to read the notes and view the programme, and up to 30 minutes for the first related activity)

Before viewing

This programme looks at a series of British TV advertisements for domestic electrical appliances which was shown during the early 1990s. The advertisments were very successful in attracting public attention, largely because of the use of cartoon-style animals and birds, instead of the customary enthusiastic humans, to praise the product. The most attractive features were the blend of original animation and regional accents, and the relaxed atmosphere. The dialogue was presented in the form of a friendly everyday conversation between family members and friends, in which the viewer was included, instead of a high-pressure sales drive. (You can compare them with an earlier style of advertising which is also shown in TV 4.) The dialogue was so arranged that there was a touch of humour, both deliberate and unintentional, in the creatures' comments. This was underlined by the balance of human and animal behaviour in the conduct of the screen characters – typical of characters in children's books and folk-tales – and by the contrast between the type of creature portrayed and the words of the speaker, for example a tortoise who described himself as an athlete (an echo of the fable of the hare and the tortoise having a race?).

You will see the highly complex and lengthy process of creating the animations and of fitting the exaggerated mouth movements to the spoken words. TV 4 will also direct your attention to the use of speech, in counterpoint to the visual presentation. The notes below will help you to relate your viewing to the discussion of artistic language use in the course book chapters. Notice the regional accent of TV 4's narrator; how does this relate to the usual narrative style of TV documentaries, and to the points made about the choice of regional accents for the speakers in the advertisements?

As you watch the programme, think about the way in which the speech of ordinary people is turned into a TV script. If you are familiar with regional accents in Britain, try also to identify the different regional accents used by the creatures. If you can't place them precisely, assign them to a general regional and social context. Think about why these voices should be chosen and whether they fit with the type of creature they are assigned to. Are there any other distinctive features about the forms of speech used, e.g. specifically women's style (see Chapter 1 of the course book)? It is useful to consider how far our appreciation of these advertisements depends on the viewer's awareness of (British) cultural assumptions about regional accent and also about the creatures who are given this variety of speech. If you are not familiar with these varieties of British English, how do the adverts strike you? If you have access to TV advertisements from other countries that use language in a similar way – either in English or in another language – you may like to try comparing them with the 'Creature Comforts' series. We shall take this discussion further when you come to the activities below.

There are two activities related to this programme: one (immediately below) to be carried out straight after viewing, and one to be carried out in week 15, if you have been able to record the programme.

After viewing (week 14)

(Allow about 30 minutes)

This activity is related to the discussion of editing everyday conversation to turn it into a dramatic script: you will be able to take this further when you study Audiocassette 4 Band 2.

After watching TV 4, jot down your own notes on two of the points mentioned above:

1   How has the everyday conversation of the speakers in these advertisements been turned into TV scripts? What do you think are the effects of the editing process?

2   What different accents of English are used by the speakers, and what is the purpose of using them in these advertisements? What identity does their use give to the product they advertise?

After making your own notes, you may like to compare them with mine.

1   You probably noticed the vast amount of editing that was needed to turn the initial recordings into the script for the advertisement – up to two hours reduced to a few minutes. This process has the effect of intensifying the conversation, removing the digressions, repetitions, hesitations and 'fillers' which are an integral part of everyday conversation (compare with Chapter 1 of the course book) but which are distractions from the functions of this script. They would lose the viewer's interest, they wouldn't help in promoting the product, and they would also prove very expensive – in TV advertising, time costs money!

This editing has foregrounded what are seen as the essential features of the conversation – the warm, family atmosphere, the easy interchanges, the individual characteristics which are exaggerated by the editing process (for example, the character of the tortoise), the touches of humour, as when the child drops a plate – in short, a concentrated essence of the conversation. It operates on a double level; it is meant to appear as ordinary conversation, but it demonstrates the 'art' of concealing art, as it has been carefully intensified to be even more typical of 'real life' than real life itself. Compare this with dramatists' methods of creating dialogue for the stage, as shown in section 5.3 of Chapter 5, and in any plays or TV films you know.

> You will be able to compare the activity in 'Creature Comforts' with Brad Bradstock's editing process (Audiocassette 4 Band 2) in making a dramatic script from Hawtin Mundy's spoken memories.

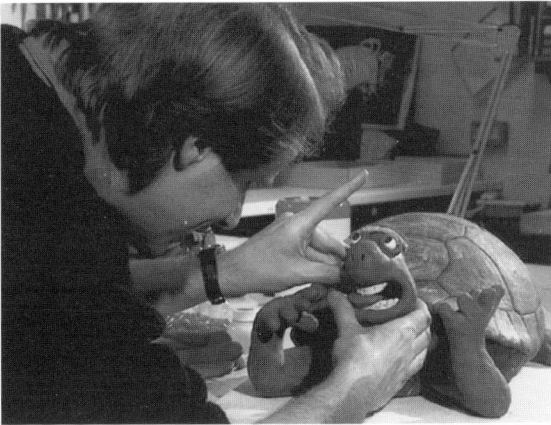

2   The social and regional accents of the speakers are one of the most appealing features of these advertisements. A range of British accents was used, with the significant exception of Received Pronunciation (RP). Why is this one omitted? How far is this an attempt to appeal to 'ordinary' British people and create the impression of a shared speech community with a common interest in household comfort and economy? You can compare this with the forms of speech used in the 1960s advertisements also shown in TV 4. Regional accents were confined to the consumers, while the product was promoted by RP speakers. Is the use of nothing but regional vernaculars aiming to suggest the democratization of the product, so that viewers will be encouraged to think that 'we' are telling each other about it, not having views imposed on us from above?

> Compare this use of regional accents with Reading A of Chapter 5 and what it says about the functions of vernacular speech in literature. You could also look back to Week 7 Block 2, with its discussion of our reaction to different accents; this will throw further light on the responses that the advertisers want us to make to their advertisements, and so to their product. Also notice TV 4's comments on the use of Johnny Morris's voice to read the final caption.

TV 4 review (week 15)

(Allow about 30 minutes)

After you have worked through section 6.7 of Chapter 6, which deals with advertisements, we recommend that you watch the programme again with the chapter's ideas in mind.

Ask yourself: what is the importance of the form of this advertisement to the way in which it gets its message across?

Notice how the element of performance is present and necessary in these advertisments. To judge its significance try the following activity:

• Transcribe the words of one of the advertisements featured in the programme. What methods have you used for representing the accent used by the speakers?

• Look back at the phonetic symbols used to transcribe speech (*Describing Language* Chapter 2) and at the ways in which the writers in Reading B of

Chapter 5 represented the accents of their speakers. How would these different transcription conventions affect your reading of a transcription?

- Now look at the words you have written, as they appear on the page. Do they have the same impact on you when you simply read them as they do when they are heard as part of the TV advertisements? If not, how much of their effect depends on the sound of the speakers' voices, the intonation, the setting, the characters given to the chosen animals or birds, the animation techniques and any other elements of the presentation? (You could compare this with your examination of the non-verbal elements of storytelling in Band 4 of the video.)

Look out also for the element of language play in the wording of the final caption of each advertisement, and the graphic design suggesting the connection between the words used and the use of electric power in the home. Finally, how far is the element of 'play' reflected in the overall design of these advertisements? What do they have in common with the comedy routines discussed in section 6.2 of Chapter 6?

AUDIOCASSETTE 4

Producers: *Anne Diack* and *Paul Manners*

Academic consultants: *Janet Maybin* and *Neil Mercer*

Band 1   Introduction to language and art

Contributors: *Janet Maybin* and *Neil Mercer* from the Open University

(Study time: about 5 minutes)

Janet Maybin and Neil Mercer, members of the course team, introduce the themes and bands of this cassette. There are no further study notes for this band.

Band 2   The art of spontaneous speech

Contributors: *Neil Mercer* from the Open University, *Melvyn Bragg*, writer and broadcaster, *Hawtin Mundy* and *Brad Bradstock*, actor

(Duration: 8 minutes; study time about 40 minutes)

This band brings together Chapter 1 and Chapter 5 of the course book. It is concerned with the use of ordinary, everyday language as art, and how this use differs in style and function from everyday conversation.

There are two parts to the band: a discussion of a radio 'talk show'; and a spontaneous and performed narration of the same event. The notes take you through each part in turn, but since the band is fairly short you may prefer to listen to the whole thing first and then replay, focusing on the questions in the notes.

A radio talk show

Neil Mercer interviews Melvyn Bragg, who is both a writer and the presenter of British TV and radio programmes connected with the arts. They discuss the radio programme *Start the Week*, a regular chat show which Melvyn Bragg chairs on BBC Radio 4.

Melvyn Bragg

Before listening

Throughout this short interview the emphasis is on spontaneous talk as an art form; you will notice the initial reference to a 'talk show' or 'chat show' as an art form in itself. As you listen, note down:

- the explanation given for the conventions of this genre;
- the editoral role Melvyn Bragg takes in helping to create the show;
- the explanation he gives for the occasions when this formula fails to work.

After listening

You will have heard Melvyn Bragg explain that he views the show as an artificial construction. Though it is based on everyday conversation, and gives the impression of being unguided, he keeps a controlling role as chair, moving the six speakers on to new subjects and ensuring that the talk matches what the show's audience wants. It is this element of selection and intensification, while keeping the spontaneity in the unscripted dialogue, which helps to make it 'art' and entertainment. Melvyn Bragg claims that this makes the chat show a distinctive use of language, different from that used, for example, in a university seminar. The one type of person who doesn't fit in is an academic who arrives expecting to read a prepared script, which belongs to the wrong genre and prevents others from joining in. We could say that it spoils the 'spontaneity' which is an important aspect of the chat show.

Are these characteristics shared with other forms of more everyday conversation? What does it mean, for instance, to say that someone is a 'good conversationalist'? Or that they are quite 'entertaining' when they speak?

Spontaneous and performed speech

The next part of this band offers two parallel narrations.

The first is Hawtin Mundy, recording his wartime experiences for an oral history project in Milton Keynes, in the south of England.

The second is an actor, Brad Bradstock. He has reworked Hawtin Mundy's spoken memories into a script for a one-man show, and we hear an extract from this.

Brad Bradstock

Before listening

We suggest that you play through the extracts, noting down the features that distinguish the spontaneous version from the scripted dramatization. What has the actor done to the original version to turn it into a performance?

(Note: the DCM is the Distinguished Conduct Medal given by the British army to non-commissioned officers and private soldiers who have distinguished themselves in action; a Maxim gun is a type of early machine gun.)

After listening

The two men had a different purpose in using the same material. The first speaker is reminiscing about his past; the other is creating a theatrical event. You probably picked out the rather rambling structure of the original memories, the pauses, linked by 'er', the digression (e.g. about such guns now being in a museum), the movement back and forth as he repeats that the gun was stripped, the admission that he has forgotten some details, and the seeming lack of connection between the incidents – the soldier just loosed off the belt of ammunition, then came the unexpected award of the DCM. In the actor's version, the narration has been tightened up, shortened and structured much more firmly ('shaped' was the first word that came to my mind). A similar vernacular accent is used, and there is apparently the same slow pace, but the hesitations and digression have gone.

The most significant part is the changing of the order in which the incidents are narrated. The unexplained award of the DCM comes first in the dramatization, and this shapes the whole narration and gives it purpose. This restructuring fits the contrast of 'fabula' and 'sjuzhet' explained in section 5.3 of Chapter 5. In the first version, 'fabula' and 'sjuzhet' work side by side, as events are narrated in the order in which they occurred in time. The dramatized version creates a tension between logical order and the order in which the events are presented to us, with the exciting incident of the award of the medal (which happens last) being told first to catch our attention and lead us through the events that caused it. The structure is so unobtrusively tight and firm, and the material so carefully selected to give only the most significant highlights, that the actor has the time to explain why the medal was awarded. Both extracts take the same length of time, 1 minute 50 seconds. Hawtin Mundy did eventually explain the reason in his recording, but he took too long in reaching this point for all of his account to be included on the audiocassette.

Compare your notes on TV 4 with this idea of the selection and intensification of ordinary speech to construct verbal art. The same techniques of editing were used there in the creation of a script for a popular series of advertisements.

Band 3   English in popular song

Contributors: *Neil Mercer*, from the Open University, and *Guy Cook*, Institute of Education, University of London

(Duration: 14 minutes; study time: about 45 minutes)

This band features seven twentieth-century popular songs, which relate to Chapter 6 of course book 2.

Before listening

Guy Cook

You will hear the following songs, in this order:

'(What a) Wonderful World' – Sam Cooke (1950s)

'Don't Fence Me In' – Bing Crosby and the Andrews Sisters (1940s)

'Around and Around' – Chuck Berry (1958)

'Masters of War' – Bob Dylan (1960s)

'Twist and Shout' – The Beatles (1960s)

'Eleanor Rigby' – The Beatles (1960s)

'Mind Over Matter' – Ice T (1990s)

In between each extract you will hear Neil Mercer and Guy Cook in a brief discussion of how the song uses the English language as part of its effect. As you listen to the band, make brief notes on:

- How important are the words in each instance, compared with the music and the element of performance?

  You could set this out in tabular form, like this:

Song	Words	Music	Performance
(What a) Wonderful World			
Don't Fence Me In			

- What does this suggest about the nature of popular song and its audience?
- What varieties of English are used in the different songs?

This third point is important in relation to the role of popular songs in the world-wide diffusion of English.

After listening

Answers to the first two points will show the continuum of popular song. I expect that you rated the Bing Crosby song as important from the point of view of words. Bob Dylan's protest song took its words seriously also, although the purpose of these words, with their denunciation of war and warmongering, was very different. The later Beatles song 'Eleanor Rigby' also emphasizes its words – we are meant to hear the striking metaphors and notice the details, though the melody and arrangement are integral parts of its effect. Ice T's 1990s rap also places an emphasis on words; it approaches a poem spoken against a musical background. The function again affects the form; rhythm and verbal effects are foregrounded, rather than a message which lies in the meaning of the words. Where does that place the other songs? Perhaps you would group Chuck Berry with the early Beatles' 'Twist and Shout' – both heavily dependent on the performance element. 'Wonderful World' has something of a balance between interacting elements of song, music and performance.

The last point highlights the influence of American pronunciation which is clear in this selection. In several songs, we hear the voices of black traditions (often imitated by white singers) and the smoother finish of the Crosby song is reminiscent of Hollywood musicals. The early Beatles song has a transatlantic influence, although as they developed they allowed their native Liverpool accent to become more prominent. As popular music today is disseminated as part of a worldwide youth culture, one of the predominant varieties of English that it takes to its listeners and imitators is American English. Think back to Peter Trudgill's research on pronunciation in popular songs, in Chapter 8 of the first course book; remember how Trudgill refers to such changing pronunciations adopted by singers as 'acts of identity'.

Band 4   The English canon

Contributors: *Marilyn Butler* has taught English literature at both Oxford and Cambridge Universities and is now Rector of Exeter College, Oxford; *Stuart Hall*, who grew up in the Caribbean, is now Professor of Sociology at the Open University; *Paul Seaver* is a Reader at Stanford University, California, and was involved in designing their 'Cultures, ideas and values' programme

(Duration: 7 minutes; study time: about 40 minutes)

The band is associated with Chapter 7 of the course book and its discussion of the canon of English writings.

Before listening

On this band you will hear three speakers, all connected with the academic world, giving contrasting views about the English canon. They explain what the canon means to them, and why their experience has led them to take this view. As you listen, jot down the views expressed by each speaker, and their reasons for regarding the canon in this light. You will find this helpful in extending your awareness of the various sides of this question, as expressed in Chapter 7.

After listening

You will have heard Marilyn Butler speak in support of the idea of a canon as a bonding force among people who share a common pool of loved literature and can respond to references to it, as to other shared cultural texts such as fairy tales. She feels that it is a problem for the USA not to have such a shared pool. (Compare this with the attitude of E.D. Hirsch Jr in section 7.6 of Chapter 7.)

Stuart Hall's Caribbean upbringing has given him a different perspective. The literature of the English canon does not reflect the physical or cultural environment in which he grew up; he is interested in what is left out of the traditional canon. His view is not hostile, like some of the writers quoted in Chapter 7; he sees the creation of an exclusive canon as one of the ways in which cultures operate. You will hear Stuart Hall giving more of his views on the relationship of language varieties to literature on Band 5.

Another perspective is given by Paul Seaver. He sees the traditional Eurocentric canon as failing to address the experience of Americans, who are composed of many cultural groups. He is involved in the Stanford course, described in Chapter 7 section 7.6 as an attempt to get rid of canons not to create a new one. Look back to the account of the Stanford course in Chapter 7. How far do you think such a move could succeed? Is any naming of specific texts as culturally important going to create a new canon anyway?

Band 5   A tongue, for sighing

Contributors: *Liz Lochhead*, poet; *Tony Harrison*, poet; *David Rubadira*, writer; *Catherine Lim*, writer; *Stuart Hall*, Open University academic; *Louise Bennett*, poet and writer

(Duration: 13 minutes; study time: about 55 minutes)

Before listening

This band goes with Chapter 8, 'A tongue, for sighing'. On it, you will hear six writers discussing their use of English in their work, and their attitudes to using English. Three of the contributions, by the first, second and last speakers, are poems concerned with the use of vernacular forms of English. The other speakers talk about the significance of English for them as a means of written expression. This band will add to the range of attitudes and views about the use of English for literary writing that you have met in Chapter 8. As you listen to it, note down how the ideas of each speaker fit with, or contrast with, the writers' views given in the chapter. Also listen for the codeswitching which forms a vital part of the three poems' structure and message. This band will give further examples of the varieties of English in use for literary purposes. How many of these poems, and of

Catherine Lim

the ones quoted in Chapter 8, would find a place in a traditional canon? You may find it easier to stop the tape between each speaker.

Liz Lochhead is a Scottish poet who uses Scots and English to great effect in her poems. (You saw Liz Lochhead on TV 1 and TV 2.)

Tony Harrison, whom you have already heard on Audiocassette 2, is a poet from Leeds, in the north of England; he refers to his Yorkshire origins in his poems.

David Rubadira is an East African writer, born in Malawi and educated in Uganda, who chooses to write in English.

Catherine Lim, who also contributed to TV 1, and whom you will see again on TV 5, is a writer of short stories who lives in Singapore and is interested in ways of adapting English to reflect her own culture.

Stuart Hall, whom you have already heard on Band 4 talking about the canon, reflects here on the cultural significance for Caribbean writers of using English.

Louise Bennett (another contributor to TV 1) is a Jamaican poet and writer, who writes in Jamaican Creole and English. Her writing illustrates the points made by Stuart Hall and by the Caribbean writers quoted in Chapter 8.

Liz Lochhead's poem 'Kidspoem/Bairnsang' is written in Scots and English and Louise Bennett's poem 'Country Bwoy' is written mainly in Jamaican Creole. The text of both poems is reproduced below to make them easier to follow (on the audiocassette you can hear the whole of 'Kidspoem/Bairnsang' and extracts from 'Country Bwoy').

Kidspoem/Bairnsang
by Liz Lochhead
It wis January
and a gey dreich day
the first day I went to the school
so
ma Mum happed me up in ma good navyblue nap coat
wi the rid tartan hood
birled a scarf aroon ma neck
pu'ed on ma pixie and ma pawkies
it wis that bitter
said
'noo ye'll no starve'
gied me a wee kiss and a kidoan skelp on the bum
and sent me off across the playground
to the place I'd learn to say
'It was January
and a really dismal day
the first day I went to school
so
my Mother wrapped me up in my best navyblue top coat
with the red tartan hood
twirled a scarf around my neck
pulled on my bobble-hat and mittens
it was so bitterly cold
said
"now you won't freeze to death"
gave me a little kiss and a pretend slap on the bottom
and sent me off across the playground
to the place I'd learn to forget to say
"It wis January

and a gey dreich day
the first day I went to the school
so
ma Mum happed me up in ma good navyblue nap coat
wi the rid tartan hood
birled a scarf aroon ma neck
pu'ed on ma pixie and ma pawkies
it was that bitter."'
Oh,
saying it was one thing
but when it came to writing it
in black and white
the way it had to be said
was as if
you were grown up, posh, male, English and dead.
(Lochhead, McGough and Olds, 1995, pp. 61–2)

Country Bwoy
by Louise Bennett
Me no like tung at all, at all!
Me no gwine go back deh.
De one no mo week me spen deh
Me meet crosses, eh-eh!

One day me walk dung King Street, an
Me go eena one store
– Me tink dem call i 'Enterprise'
But me is not so sure.

Me tan up tan up bout de place
Look pon everyting
Tell me see one oman queeze sinting
And me hear de sinting ring.

Me see one doorway open, de
Oman go tru de door.
Me ax one man a whe she gawn
An him seh up Five Prize Store.

Me tink to meself 'Ah doan know
Whe Five Prize deh, but tan!
Ef de sinting cya har deh, it can
Cya me a foreign lan.'

Me member Lou whe gawn a sea
From me was a li bwoy
– Ah seh 'Ah gwine go look fi har'
An me heart full up wid joy.

Me put me han pon de button,
De door open wid ease,
Me step een an seh to de man
'Stap me at Cuba, please.'

De man meck up him face dis lacka
When it set fi rain
So tun roun ax me ef me tink
Me eena aeroplane.

De ting start move, me feel like me
Drink bout twelve glass a beer,
Ah never know meself so-tell
De man seh 'Come out here'.

Ah step eena one pretty place.
Ah nearly drop a grung
When ah see de straight-hair ladies
Jus walking up an dung.

One pretty gal step up so seh
'What can I do for you?'
Hear me: 'Dis is Cuba, I presume.
Ah waan see Cousin Lou.'

De gal bus out a laugh an seh
'You're dizzy from de ride.
You're from de country? Oh, poor ting!
Jus step aroun dis side.'

She show me some step so seh 'Don't
Ride on de lif no more.'
Me go dung forty step, an lan
Same place back eena de store.

Me pass boot, hat on claht, me go
Een an come outa door,
But all de tun me tun an twis
Me still eena de store.

Massa, me get eena temper,
Ah teck a oat an seh
Ah doan like tung at all at all
An ah hooden gu back deh.

(Morris (ed.), 1982, pp. 11–13)

We can also think back to Video Band 4 which we worked on in weeks 14 and 15. Jan Blake chose to use Jamaican Creole as an appropriate variety for telling her Anansi story; she switched into it for the Caribbean story, after an initial explanation in a variety of English spoken in the north west of England, closer to the British standard. She also used this variety when explaining to the audience the pronunciation they needed for the song. (She uses both forms in daily life, speaking Creole with other Creole-speaking friends and sometimes with family members.) You may like to replay Band 4 and listen for these switches.

Band 6   *Lost in Translation*

Contributor: *Eva Hoffman,* writer
(Duration: 13 minutes; study time: about 25 minutes)

Before listening

You have already met Eva Hoffman's work in Chapter 8. On this band you have the opportunity to hear her read more of her work and reflect on her experiences in coming to terms with English as a language for writing and constructing an identity.

As you listen to this band, note down:

- her reasons for choosing English as her writer's language;
- the difference she experiences between the uses of English and Polish and what the two languages mean to her;
- how her attitude compares with that of the other writers quoted in Chapter 8 and on Band 5.

After listening

You may have seen parallels between Eva Hoffman's choice of English and that of some of the speakers in TV 3 who came to the USA as immigrants. If you read nineteenth-century English literature, you may also have thought of Joseph Conrad, another Polish writer who made his name from his novels, written in his adopted language of English and approved as 'English culture' by the traditionalist 1930s constructors of the canon of English literature!

One of the interesting points that you will have noticed is Eva Hoffman's adoption of another language and her refusal to use her native Polish as a language for her writings. Coming to English from outside, she adopts the standard variety as the language of her new identity. Unlike some immigrants, she does so freely and without a feeling of strong cultural tension, but she admits that at first English was the language of thoughts, not of emotions. She describes how she grew into the use of English as a language for feelings.

This band is a bridge between Block 4, concerned with the uses of English as art, and the topics of Blocks 5 and 6. In studying them, you will move on to look at the learning of English, both as a first language and in multilingual settings. The material of week 17 will be valuable as you go on to this area of study.

VIDEO

Band 4 Storytelling (from video page 215)

Producer: *Anne Diack*

Academic consultant: *Joan Swann*; we are grateful to *David Sutcliffe* for advice on Jamaican storytelling

Main contributor: *Jan Blake*, storyteller

(Duration: approximately 11 minutes; study times: week 14 – 1 hour, week 15 – 1 hour 30 minutes)

This band gives us an example of one form of 'language as art'; we see and hear a storyteller entertaining her audience with a traditional story. We shall be asking you to study several different aspects of the band. In particular, we shall be thinking about the way in which the language is organized to create a story and the use of verbal and non-verbal communication to tell it effectively to an audience. In week 14 we shall concentrate on the structure of the story, and on the storyteller's ways of telling it. In later weeks, we shall return to the audience's participation and its importance, the use of verbal and non-verbal means of narration and the variety of English that she chooses to use.

The story: this is a folk-tale featuring Anansi (or Anancy), a well-known figure in Caribbean and West African stories. He usually takes the form of a spider, who uses his wits to get himself out of trouble and defeat the stronger animals who surround him. He is an ambivalent figure, clever and amusing but also showing less admirable characteristics such as greed and deceit; his audience is meant to enjoy his adventures but not necessarily to admire his methods. While these stories have many uniquely Caribbean features, they share similarities with the folk-tales of other cultures, such as talking animals with human characteristics. Anansi himself has parallels in other figures who share his ability to succeed by intelligence or cunning where greater strength or power fails.

The storyteller. Jan Blake was born in Manchester, England; her parents had come to England from Jamaica. Her family did not have a tradition of telling folk stories – she first came across Anansi stories when she joined a storytelling group, Common Lore, in 1986. Here she met Irish, African and Caribbean stories, some of which she included in her repertoire as a storyteller. Although her stories were originally part of a tradition of oral 'tellings', she first got to know them through reading and research; the story you see on the video came from *Jamaican Song and Story*, a collection made by Walter Jekyll in 1907, and she has also collected stories from the taped archive of traditional material at the Afro-Caribbean oral history centre in Jamaica.

Although the outline of the story was learnt in this way, Jan does not rehearse it word for word beforehand. Each story builds up its own rhythm and form from repeated telling, but every performance has its own differences, depending on the context and audience. Jan says that the audience is very important; it is the reason why the story is told. While she does not consciously adapt her style, as a performer she responds to their reception of the story.

The recording: the video was recorded at a storytelling session at the Open University's central campus at Milton Keynes in 1995, before an invited audience. This took place in a former church, now used for concerts and performances. Jan told three traditional Caribbean stories and one from Nigeria; her performance was recorded live.

As you watch and listen to the story, you will be struck by a number of features – the rhythm of the telling, the lively acting out of the different characters' ways of speaking, the Creole which Jan uses as an appropriate variety for this Jamaican story, and the enjoyment of the performance by both teller and audience.

Watch the whole band once through first, to gain the experience of the storytelling; you may like to see it more than once, in case you missed any points in the story. Try to imagine that you are part of the audience. Join in, if you like, with their responses; the song, in particular, is very catchy – I caught myself singing it for days after I first saw this band. If you have (or know) young children, you may like to watch it with them, and notice how they respond to it.

After viewing (week 14)

We suggest you focus initially on the narrative techniques used by Jan; and then on aspects of the song as performance. The notes below will help with this.

Narrative techniques

We shall be using this band as a practical example of the approaches to language that are examined in Block 4. Chapter 5 of the course book discusses the linguistic devices that creative writers use to create verbal art, such as dialogue, narrative structure, original uses of words and rhythmic patterns of speech. Think back over Jan's story; watch the band again, if you like, to help you remember how she told the story. As you do so, make brief notes on her narrative techniques, and on the typical features that help us to recognize this as a traditional folk-story, even though we may not be familiar with the culture from which it comes. Look for:

- how she begins the story;
- the use of dialogue;

- rhythmic structure in sentences, and use of repetition;
- how the story is ended.

My notes on the narrative follow; but please carry out your own analysis before reading these.

You will probably have recognized one of the best known of traditional folk-tale openings, 'Once upon a time ...' which is also used in folk-stories told in British English. We shall return later to the call to draw the audience's attention, 'Anansi' and their response 'Story', a typical way of opening a Caribbean story of this kind.

This formula alerts the audience to the type of narrative that they can expect to follow. Within the folk-tale framework, conventional reality is suspended, so that a tiger who can take off his fur to go swimming and a trickster who teaches songs to the monkeys and escapes by climbing up his own spider-web are acceptable characters.

Section 3.3 of Chapter 5 discusses the construction of dialogue; Jan uses it to vary the narrative and give the characters individual personalities – the cunning Anansi, the haughty Brer Tiger, the chattering monkeys. It is used in a stylized manner; we would not expect realistic dialogue between animals.

Repetition and rhythm are evident both in the characters' speeches and in the narration. There are plenty of examples to choose from: for example, the 'it was hot, hot, hot ...' with which the story begins; the combination of rhythm and repetition in 'all of that fur and all of that fat', balanced by Brer Tiger's 'I am supposed to have fur and I am supposed to have fat'; the list of parts of Brer Tiger's body from which he rolls down his fur and peels off his fat; the cumulative repetition when Anansi uses first one finger to taste the fat, then more; the vivid phrase 'wheel and fling' as Brer Tiger attacks the monkeys and then suffers the same fate himself. You probably noticed plenty of others. Such devices help to give the story its structure and build up to climaxes within the story.

The conclusion, like the opening, uses a traditional formula. Jan uses one of the endings of the Caribbean tradition, 'Jack Mandora said it, not me'; Jack Mandora, the keeper of Heaven's door, has to be informed that the storyteller does not approve of all Anansi's tricks, however entertaining they may be. Louise Bennett, in her introduction to Jekyll's *Jamaican Sons*, remembered that all the listeners had to say, 'Jack Mandora, me no choose none', to show that they also did not approve of his cunning ways.

As you listened, you were probably reminded of similar examples from other traditional stories; in British tales, there is the formulaic repetition of 'Who's been eating *my* porridge?' in the story of 'Goldilocks and the three bears', for example.

You may like to spend a few moments noting down features of traditional stories and storytelling with which you are familiar, and comparing them with those you observed in this story. Look back also to pages 231–4 of *Describing Language* and see how far this story fits with the schema of traditional stories with which you are familiar through your own cultural tradition.

The story as performance

This is a spoken performance, not a written story for us to read silently to ourselves, so we are now going to turn our attention to the oral element and its significance. Read the transcribed extract below – it is the first section of the story. Then make brief notes comparing it with the performed version on pages 231–51 of the video. What are the main differences between the two versions? Is anything added in performance, or lost in transcription?

Transcribed extract, pages 231–51

Once upon a time, it was hot, hot, hot – hot like fire, hotter than today, hotter than July – and Anansi and Brer Tiger decided dem want to go and swim in Blue Hole. Blue Hole was a very nice, cool, deep piece of water, under the shade of banana trees. So, Anansi and Brer Tiger went to Blue Hole. And Brer Tiger was just about to dive into the water, when Anansi said:

'Brer Tiger, Brer Tiger, Brer Tiger, Brer Tiger! Do not dive into the water, with all of that fur and all of that fat, because if you dive in with all of that fur and all of that fat you will sink like a stone and drown!'

Brer Tiger said: 'Anansi, I am a tiger. I am supposed to have fur, and I am supposed to have fat – so don't tell me no rubbish, I'm going to swim.'

'Brer Ti-, Brer Tiger,' said Brer Anansi, 'Do not dive into the water! Imagine how your wife would feel, if you drown in that water! Imagine how your children would feel if you drown in that water! Brer Tiger, as your best friend I beg you, don't, don't dive in. Take off your fur, and take off your fat.'

Brer Tiger said: 'You mean I have to really take off me –'

Him say, 'Yes, take off your fur, and take off your fat.'

'All right,' said Brer Tiger, and him start to peel off the fur, off him face – roll it up, pull it off him ears and then roll it down the back of the neck …

My own notes on this follow – please read them after you have made your own comparison between the written and spoken texts.

Some of the features that you probably included are:

- The effects created by the storyteller's use of her voice – for example, the rhythm and intonation of her phrases, the stress that she gave to certain important words, the changes in pitch and tone by which she differentiated the speech of the characters, the changes in pace and volume through which she controlled the development of the action and built up the excitement – you may have thought of other aspects of the use of her voice;
- The use of non-verbal communication. You have already been asked, this week, to read section 6.2 of *Describing Language*, which discusses the different aspects of non-verbal methods of communicating; some of these, especially gesture, posture and body orientation, facial expression and gaze, are very much in evidence as significant parts of Jan's performance. We shall return to this aspect in week 15.
- The appearance and physical presence of the storyteller. This is closely linked with another aspect that we shall return to next week: the presence of a live audience and their responses, both spontaneous and encouraged by Jan. On the video we are aware of the presence of an audience, and the setting of the performance, which give us the context for this particular storytelling.

The creation of the transcipt presented its own issues of deciding what form and conventions to use in representing this nonstandard speech. We could have attempted to use spelling conventions which emphasize Jamaican pronunciation and grammar (for examples of such conventions see the transcript of Guyanese Creole in the study guide to Block 1, and the folk-tale from Cameroon on page 183 of Chapter 5, which you read this week). However, we wanted to concentrate on the narrative structure rather than the characteristics of this particular variety of English, so we opted for a more 'neutral' spelling. You may like to try your own transcription, using a nonstandard spelling which is closer to the pronunciation of the original. Another alternative, of course, would be a totally phonetic transcription, but this isn't easy to read without considerable practice; you could try this, too, if you've become interested in phonetics.

You may also like to look back at Reading B of Chapter 5 to remind yourself of how some writers have tackled the question of representing nonstandard varieties of English in writing.

Further analysis (week 15)

This week we are returning to the Anansi story to look at those aspects of the band which help us in understanding the element of play and performance in English as 'art' which is this week's study topic. The notes below will help you make a more detailed analysis of Jan's use of her voice, aspects of non-verbal communication and the role of the audience.

The voice in storytelling

We would like you to return to the short transcribed extract and the equivalent section of the video band. Play pages 231–51 again, this time making notes on the ways in which the voice is used, and the manner of delivery, and how these relate to the actual words of the story. Focus on intonation (check this by re-reading pages 50–64 in section 2.4 of *Describing Language*, if you like), overall changes in pitch (e.g. from higher to lower), alterations in pace (faster or slower), stress on particular words and phrases, and interesting changes in the tone and quality of the voice. In each case, ask yourself *why* these changes occur, and whether they help in conveying the meaning of the story. There are many ways in which you could arrange your notes. The conventions that you have met in *Describing Language* for representing different aspects of speech may not be the best to use here, as you are looking for a number of features at once. You may like to try using columns, like the example below:

Transcript	*Features*	*Possible effects*
And Brer Tiger was just about to dive into the water when Anansi said	slower pace from just about; slight degree of pitch raising on just about; lower pitch at beginning of into the water	Is this Brer Tiger teetering on the edge – before diving?
Brer Tiger Brer Tiger Brer Tiger Brer Tiger	faster pace, higher pitch, slight increase in volume	Change of delivery gives character own distinctive voice; sense of urgency created

You could also try a more graphic method of representation, if you like – it could be interesting to try this after, or instead of, the column method.

BRERTIGERBRERTIGERBRERTIGERBRERTIGER

Anansi said   do not dive into the water with all of that fur and all of that fat because if you dive in with all of that fur and all of that faT you will

sink like a

stone and

drown

Non-verbal and verbal communication

We will now look at the non-verbal elements of Jan's performance and how they work with and support the speech, picking up the point that we made last week. Look back briefly at section 6.2 of *Describing Language* to remind yourself of the main forms of non-verbal communication that have been identified. Haptics are not very relevant in this case, nor are proxemics, in that Jan does not change her nearness to the audience to any great extent. Had she done so, or reached out to touch a member of the audience, it would have become a very different type of performance. If you have ever attended a theatre where the actors come down into the audience and make contact with them you will realize that it can be quite exciting but disturbing as the expected conventions of the performance have been broken.

We shall concentrate in particular on: gesture, to see if it adds emphasis; facial expression as a means of conveying emotion; posture and body movements. Gaze and eye contact are also important, but it is difficult to analyse these precisely from this type of recording.

Re-watch the band from Jan's first call of 'Anansi' to the end of the transcribed extract, focusing on what these types of non-verbal behaviour add to the story. You will need to pause and replay sequences, as it is difficult to take everything in at a single viewing. If your videoplayer allows you to play the recording in slow motion, or to advance frame by frame, try this with sequences that seem particularly interesting. Looking at a short sequence frame by frame will illustrate the very precise coordination of verbal and non-verbal elements.

We suggest you look carefully at:

- how gesture and posture are used in the first interaction between Jan and the audience, to mark Jan's turn and to bring the audience in;
- how gesture is used to give emphasis in the opening section of the story, and to help in creating the setting;
- how Jan uses non-verbal as well as verbal means to animate the characters, especially posture and facial expression.

Try transcribing one or two phrases, using a column transcript. Write the speech in the left-hand column, and note associated non-verbal features in the right-hand column. How do the verbal and non-verbal elements seem to work together?

When you have tried out your own analysis, compare this with the notes below. Some examples of verbal and non-verbal features working together that we noticed are:

Blue Hole was a very nice, cool, deep piece of water, under the shade of banana trees	Gesture of hands making a canopy of leaves (see photographs (a)–(c))
And Brer Tiger was just about to dive into the water	Jan bends forward as though diving (see photographs (d)–(h))
'Brer Tiger, Brer Tiger ... sink like a stone and drown!'	Jan, as Anansi, warns Brer Tiger – leaning slightly forward, worried expression (see photograph (i); note the use of pointing gestures to mark the repetition of 'all of that fur and all of that fat')
Brer Tiger said, 'Anansi, I am a tiger ... I'm going to swim.'	Jan as Brer Tiger – erect, disdainful expression (see photograph (j))

Cupping gesture precedes verbal phrase; Jan's hands are already in position as she begins to say 'under'; her hands are at their highest point to emphasize 'shade'.

(a)   under

(b)   the

(c)   shade

As the sequence begins, Jan bends forward then stoops down to 'dive' (her lowest point); she tilts forward slightly on the first syllable of 'into' then begins to raise her head.

(d)   and Brer Tiger

(e)   *was just about*

(f)   *to dive*

(g)   *into*

(h)   *the water*

Jan as Anansi

(i)

Jan as Brer Tiger

(j)

Extension activity: transcription and analysis

Now you can draw on these two approaches, verbal and non-verbal to see what they contribute to the total effect of another section of the performance. Select another short extract from Jan's story – choose any part that attracts you (pages 276–86 are a good example and give you plenty of chances to focus on Jan). Transcribe the words first, then watch the extract again, stopping the tape where necessary. Make notes on:

- the use of the voice;
- the use of non-verbal communication.

Then compare the two, noting where and how they support each other in helping to make the storytelling more effective.

The role of the audience

Finally this week, let us consider briefly the audience participation in the performance. Make brief notes on the extent and nature of the audience's response to the story, both spontaneously and with Jan's encouragement. My own suggestions on this follow below.

We have already noted last week that Jan herself is aware of the importance of the audience. If you have taken part in a performance of any kind yourself, or read or told stories to children, you will be aware of the impact of the audience's response, which can make or spoil a performance. In this case, the camera focuses on the audience from time to time; we see their enjoyment and amusement, and from time to time we hear their laughter. They are perhaps a little subdued, maybe because they are unfamiliar with the performer or the setting or because they are not used to this type of story. An audience for whom this was a familiar form of entertainment and who knew the performer could have responded rather more freely. Cultural context also comes in here; audiences in England are accustomed to sitting quietly during performances and often have to be coaxed, as we see Jan doing, into a louder response.

On several occasions Jan brings the audience into the action. At the beginning of the band they are singing together. When she is about to begin the story she has them responding to the traditional Caribbean call, 'Anansi' and response, 'Story'. You will have noticed how she alters the pitch of the final call into a long descending sound which they repeat. Later they are cast as characters; they become the little monkeys encouraged to reply, 'We want to learn' and coached in the appropriate pronunciation for singing the song. Were you reminded of the 'call and response' that was discussed in week 13 of Block 3? You may like to compare these elements of Jan's performance with Audiocassette 4 Band 5 where another audience is being coached in 'call and response'.

REFERENCES

LOCHHEAD, L., MCGOUGH, R. and OLDS, S. (1995) *Penguin Modern Poets*, vol. 4, Harmondsworth, Penguin, pp. 61–2.

MORRIS, M. (ed.) (1982) *Louise Bennett, Selected Poems*, Kingston, Jamaica, Sangsters Book Stores.

ACKNOWLEDGEMENTS

Grateful acknowledgement is made to the following sources for permission to reproduce material in this study guide:

Text

Lochhead, E., 1995, 'Kidspoem/Bairnsang', *Penguin Modern Poets*, Vol 4, Penguin Books, Copyright © Liz Lochhead, by permission of A. P. Watt Ltd; Bennett, L., 1982, 'Country Bwoy', in Morris, M. (ed.) *Louise Bennett Selected Poems,* Sangster's Book Stores Ltd, Kingston, Jamaica.

Photographs

Page 28: Courtesy of LWT; *page 29:* © Brad Bradstock; *page 30:* © Guy Cook.

Printed in the United Kingdom by Caligraving Limited, Thetford Norfolk

16493C/u210b2sg4i2.1